Sincere thanks to
Kari, Anne, Tim
and,
always and of course,
Patty.

Library of Congress Cataloging-in-Publication Data

Hanson, Warren.
    Raising you alone / written and illustrated by Warren Hanson.
        p. cm.
    ISBN 0-9726504-6-6 (alk. paper)
        1. Single parents. 2. Single parent families.
        3. Picture books for children. I. Title.

HQ759.915H37 2005
306.85'6—dc22   2005045995

TRISTAN Publishing
2300 Louisiana Avenue North, Suite B
Golden Valley, Minnesota 55427

Visit **www.tristanpublishing.com** for more information.

Raising You Alone

Warren Hanson

TRISTAN Publishing
Minneapolis

Let me sit here, close beside you.
You are growing up so fast!
I can't believe how you are changing
every day!
I still remember you as little.
But your little days are past.
They're like a dream.
Those days can seem so far away.

Some dreams come true.
And some dreams don't.
There was a dream that I once had
of both a mom and dad
to raise you as their own.

That happy dream did not come true.
But I am happy here with you,
and now it looks like
I'll be raising you alone.

We have some good times
and some hard times to look back on.
And I know
that we would love to keep those good times
if we could.
So let's collect the happy memories,
and make more as we go,
and let's do everything we can
to make them good.

Like...
climbing underneath the covers
on a rainy afternoon
while we watch some dumb old movie on TV.

With our chocolate milk and popcorn,
all curled up in our cocoon,
we can pretend there's no one else
but you and me.

I want to teach you how to fish,
how to do laundry, how to dance,
how to change a tire,
and how to cook and sew.

How to fix a flooding toilet,
how to iron a pair of pants.
I want to teach you all the things
that I don't know!

How to walk and run and ride a bike,
and how to drive a car.
How to travel where your heart
may take you to.

Then how to find your way back home again,
no matter where you are,
because you know that I'll be
waiting here for you.

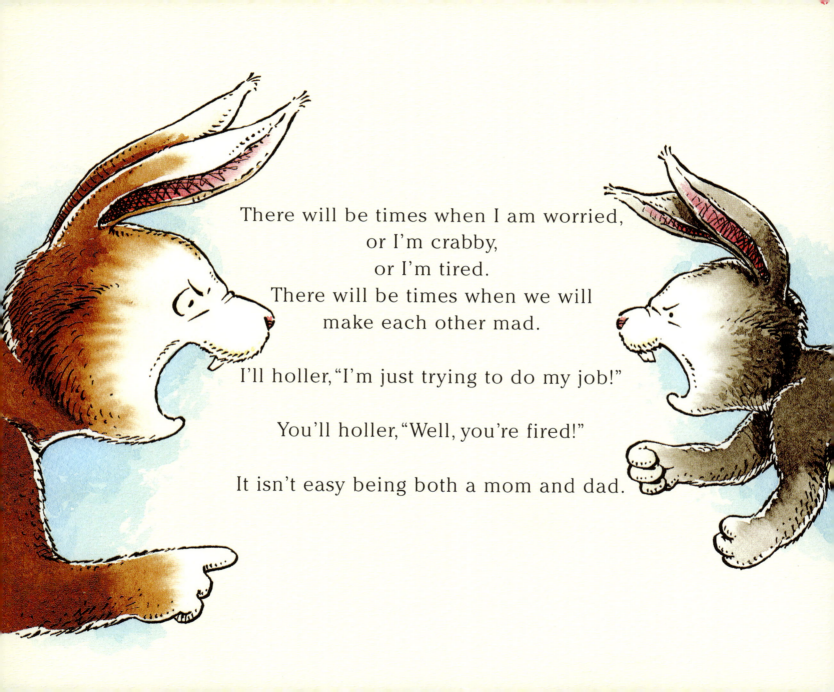

There will be times when I am worried,
or I'm crabby,
or I'm tired.
There will be times when we will
make each other mad.

I'll holler, "I'm just trying to do my job!"

You'll holler, "Well, you're fired!"

It isn't easy being both a mom and dad.

But I hope you'll hire me back,
that you'll forgive, and I will too,
so we can work together as a family.
Because from now on,
it will be my job to take good care of you,
while I do all I can to take good care of me.

Oh sure, I'll worry about money.

Will I ever have enough
to give you everything I think you'll
want or need?
Toys and books and clothes and college?
All the big and little stuff
that says I love you,
and I want you to succeed?

There will be times when you will have to be
in someone else's care —
at school, at day care,
or with Grandma, or with friends —
while I am busy doing all the things
a parent has to do.
Sometimes it seems the work and worry
never ends.

But I will be there when it matters —
cross my heart, no matter what.
If it's important to be there, I'll find a way.
Out on the field, the court, the stage —
I'll try to be there on the dot.
I want to stand and clap my hands at every play.

From your first step to your first date.
From your first tooth to your first kiss.
From your first word
until the day you say, "I do."

There's not one single thing about you
I will ever want to miss.
I want to be a part of every part of you.

But there are things you'll want to talk about
with someone else, not me.
And that's okay.
I guess that's what best friends are for.

Although I'll give you all I can
and be the best that I can be,
I understand
sometimes a friend can give you more.

Well, I may need a best friend too, some day.
A grown-up friend, I mean.
The kind of friend who understands
the grown-up stuff.
And though you know I love you so —
no one will ever come between us —
there are times, just like for you,
it's not enough.

So if this friend comes here for dinner,
don't make milk come out your nose
or make rude noises.
Say "excuse me" if you do.
You see, I'd like this friend to like me.
But no matter how it goes,
I'll never like somebody else
as much as you.

It's you and I who really matter.
It's this family that counts.
We are the very best
this world has ever known.
And so, in spite of how we got here,
it's my pleasure to announce
that we're amazing!
— though I'm raising you alone.

There isn't anyone
that I will ever love as much as you.
And so I promise you, by all the stars above,
no matter who or what or when or where
our lives may lead us to,

I will always love you.

       I will always love you.

              I will always love you.

You are a part of me, you know.
The very heart of me, you know.
You are the greatest blessing
I have ever known.
Maybe my dream did not come true,
but I am still here loving you.
Now you and I can dream a new dream,
all our own.

Until that dream comes true,
I will be raising you alone.

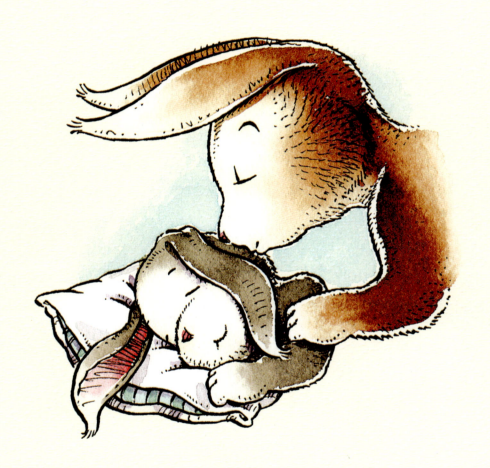